SCARY GRAPHICS

BEST FRIENDS UNTIL THE END

raintree
a Capstone company — publishers for children

Raintree is an imprint of Capstone Global Library Limited, a company incorporated in England and Wales having its registered office at 264 Banbury Road, Oxford, OX2 7DY – Registered company number: 6695582

www.raintree.co.uk
myorders@raintree.co.uk

Edited by Abby Huff
Designed by Tracy Davies and Heidi Thompson
Original illustrations © Capstone Global Library Limited 2022
Originated by Capstone Global Library Ltd

978 1 3982 3494 9

British Library Cataloguing in Publication Data
A full catalogue record for this book is available from the British Library

BEST FRIENDS UNTIL THE END

BY **STEVE FOXE**

ILLUSTRATED BY **ALAN BROWN**

WORD OF WARNING:

SCARY THINGS CAN HIDE BEHIND FRIENDLY FACES.

After school and heading home . . .

Um . . . excuse me.

Did you get locked out?

Oh, I don't—

A sleepover? That sounds like a great idea!

Later...

It was fun hanging out today. Maybe we can meet up again some—

How about a sleepover? Here? Tonight?

Mum.

Who's your new friend, honey?

I'm Lizzie.

I've just moved in upstairs. Beth has been showing me around.

Lizzie, fabulous hair! You girls look like two peas in a pod.

Yeah, and it's getting a little weird, to be honest.

Did your parents walk you down? I'd love to say hello.

Parents? Oh, yes! I have parents.

But they . . . work nights, actually.

Well, feel free to come and visit any time, then. Isn't that right, Beth?

Several hours of TV (and bowls of snacks) later . . .

YAWN

I think I'm ready for bed. You can have the bathroom first while I get the sleeping bags.

Bathroom is all yours, BFF.

Agh!

You really sneaked up on me. Wait, did you change your bottoms to match mine?

Of course not, silly. I came here in these.

Ha, oh yeah. Obviously.

I'll be back in a sec. Make yourself at home.

Okay, Beth. You finally have a friend. Why are you blowing it by getting freaked out by everything she does?

So *what* if she dresses and behaves just like you?

So what if you just met and—

Eww, what is that?

Is it the same goo from the hallway? How did it get in the bathroom?

I'm going into town, Mum.

Are you meeting up with Lizzie again?

Um, no. Not today.

You practically ran away from her this morning. That's no way to treat your *friend*.

I just . . . value my alone time.

Haven't you had enough "alone time"? It's healthy to make friends, Beth.

Yeah, Mum. I'll be back by dinner.

At the mall arcade . . .

I guess it is kind of lonely without—

Lizzie, you are so funny.

Ha, ha, ha!

Lizzie and the popular kids? What is she . . .

Camouflage. Of course. I guess she was serious about fitting in.

I don't know what you mean, Beth.

I was just making friends. Fitting in.

Our talk last night inspired me to . . . *study* other environments.

I am new here, after all.

But don't worry. You're still my very, *very* best fr—

Err, Lizzie, everything okay? You ran off so fast.

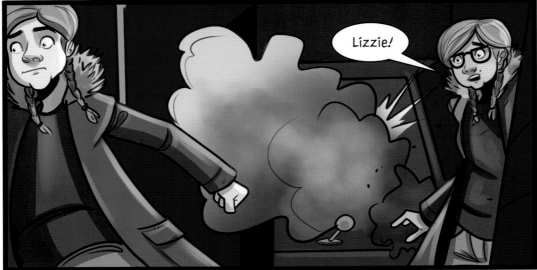

Soon, back at the flat . . .

Okay, "BFF". Something strange is happening, and I'm going to find out what.

Besides, it's time I got to know more about *you* . . .

1. In your own words, describe how Beth feels about Lizzie copying her. What makes you think that? How would you feel if a friend started dressing and behaving in the same way you did?

2. Flip back through the book and find at least three moments that hint that Lizzie isn't an ordinary girl. Make sure you look at both the text and art.

3. When Beth sneaks out and goes to Lizzie's apartment, the art uses very cool colours. Why do you think the artist made this choice? What mood does it create? How would it be different if the colouring was warmer?

4. The mysterio...
throughout th...
does it appe...
the sticky su...

5. What do you th...
Beth at the end...
she ever be see...
Lizzie do next?

THE AUTHOR

e author of more than fifty children's books and comics
ding Spider-Ham, Batman, Pokémon, Transformers,
and Steven Universe, as well as other titles in Raintree's
and Far Out Fables series. He has also written a number of
 adults . . . which you can read when you're older. He lives
 A, and is always on the lookout for strange black goo.

THE ILLUSTRATOR

 British freelance artist. He's worked on a variety of
ing Ben 10 Omniverse graphic novels for Viz Media, as well
ok illustrations for HarperCollins and Franklin Watts. He
est in the comic book world, where he's at home creating
ces. Alan works from an attic studio, along with his trusty
e miniature schnauzer, and his two sons, Wilf and Teddy.

GLOSSARY

arcade place with many games that you can play by putting a coin or token into them

camouflage something, such as the colour or pattern of fur or a special covering, that makes animals, people and objects look like the area around them

carbon chemical element that is found in all living things and is the basis for life

environment everything around a living thing that affects how it lives and grows

obsessed thinking about something all the time

popular liked by many people

second-hand having already been owned or used by someone else

snoop search out and look at private information

species group of living things that share similar features

territory all the things related to a particular activity or interest

trend newest clothing and styles worn by many people

value think that something is very important